THE
EXCHANGE

Alice A. DeWittie

THE
EXCHANGE

The Parable of The Seed

Everyone is invited...what is your response?

IGNITE
PRESS
Fresno, CA

Published in the United States by

Ignite Press
5070 N. Sixth St. #189
Fresno, CA 93710
www.IgnitePress.us

ISBN 979-8-9850033-0-7
ISBN 979-8-9850033-1-4 (ebook)

For bulk purchase and for booking, contact:

Alice A. DeWittie
info@511impact.com

Library of Congress Control Number: 2021919721

Cover and interior art by J. Brian Craig
Cover design by Kathleen Cantwell
Interior design by Michelle M. White
Edited by Emma Hatcher

To Jesus, the Author and Finisher of my faith.

Table of Contents

PART 2: *The Parable of the Seed*

Acknowledgements

To the team who cheered me on: Megan Martin who believed before I did. Patty Myers for telling me that I am "the tongue of a ready writer." Shelly Gibbs, who saw me in a field of glory. Kelley Salber, who brings out the artist in everyone. My incredible fellow explorers of the more: Cathie Sipe, Lauren Breslin, Cassie Johnson, and Shanda Harris. May we all boldly go where we've never gone before.

PART 1

The Exchange

The Allegory of the Exchange

CHAPTER 1

The Exchange

A̶ndras, Part 1

The room was bright; glimmering shafts of light beamed down from the vaulted ceiling dome, dancing off the dust in the air. Gold, brown, and yellow hues strewn themselves across the room. An autumn palate of marble counters, mahogany, accents of gold fixtures. The man strode across the room, allowing the glass doors to revolve quietly behind him. He hoped that he looked confident, knowing, bold even; but his eyes darted around, trying to get the layout, to find the quick exit. Self-conscious as he looked at his watch, then realizing the clock on the wall started the Westminster chime of high noon. Wasn't there a movie of that name? A gunfight maybe? A showdown? High noon. A time of decision.

Opening his suit jacket, he removed a pen from the inner pocket and stood at the desk, casually pulling out the slip from the pile and writing. Slowly, carefully, he signed it, in his most confident, knowing, and bold style. As he walked to the counter, he measured the others in the room. Were they somebodies or nobodies? Had they done this before, or was this their first? Were they as terrified as he? Reaching into the side pocket of his tailored slacks, he pulled out a coin, then a bill clip, then a key. Putting it all back in his pocket, his hand lingered, carefully feeling over the edges of the key; the familiar feel of each curve and bend calmed him

Now at the counter, "Hello. This is mine," passing his slip under the golden bars. The balding clerk opened the slip slowly, read it, and looked up. Everything in the man yearned for the door. His every cell started to turn and walk back.

"Ah. I see." The clerk spoke while scanning carefully the head, shoulders, and chest of the man. Without thinking, his slight step back created the distance the clerk's eyes needed for the full view.

"'This is it then?" more a statement than a question.

"Yes, that's all I have."

"All? This is all?"

"Yes." Then, with a slight intake of breath, the words betrayed him as he added "today."

"Ah. Very good. All for now. Today."

Reaching under the counter the clerk pulled out a sealed envelope, read the name on the front softly to himself, tapped the envelope on the counter, and, looking into the eyes of the man, "This is for you."

As he took the envelope, the man's eyes stared at the calligraphed writing while he nervously opened the flap. His hands started to tremble, resting his elbows on the counter to keep them still, he pulled open the ivory envelope and looked inside.

"All of this?"

"Yes, this is everything. It is your exchange."

CHAPTER 2

Her Invitation

Lydia, Part 1

Standing on the sidewalk, she examined the door: glass, brass, huge—occupying a broad swath of the entry. Looking through the revolving door, a cavernous hall beckoned, glittering, gold shafts of sun rays hitting the marble floors. She felt imposed, her attention focused and drawn to a foreign place, The Exchange. She stepped back and let the coming and going of those entering and leaving swirl around her.

As she was watching the door, a man appeared beside her. Graying temples, reading glasses folded in his pinstripe coat pocket; he said, "Can I help you?"

"Aaaah, no. I don't think so."

"Well, I noticed you've been standing here awhile. Have you been invited?"

"Invited?" she echoed, coming out of her thoughts.

"Were you called to this place?"

"Yes . . . well, maybe. I received an invitation; I don't really know who sent it."

Holding out his hand, "Ah! May I see it?"

Unaccustomed to talking to strangers in the city, yet he seemed to know exactly what she was there for. She dug through her leather work bag; past her set of home keys, makeup bag, and wallet, and finally produced a richly embossed invitation with the seal broken and her name neatly written in calligraphy on the envelope. "This came yesterday."

Unfolding the reading glasses from his pocket, he scanned the envelope and contents. "Ah, mmmm, yes, it is a personal invitation, Lydia. You can go in if you like."

"Well, I really don't know what this is all about. I've got work to do, so I think I'll be going. Thanks for your help. Have a good day." Words flying out as she turned to go.

"It is an **open** invitation, so you can enter anytime you like."Pinstripe said, retucking The Invitation back into the envelope.

"Okay, uh, just not today, thanks." She reached out to retrieve the envelope from his hand.

"Ah. Tomorrow perhaps?"

"Maybe. I mean, I, ... I'll think about it. I don't really feel like I need it, too much going on."

"Hm, you don't need it. Hmm . . ." he mused, putting his glasses back in the suit pocket.

"Thanks, have a good one." She strode away, stuffing the envelope back into her bag and reaching for her keys. Putting as much purpose in her step as she could, "I don't need it anyway. I'm fine," convincing herself as she walked away.

CHAPTER 3

Her Exchange

Lydia, Part 2

Things change.
Seasons.
Relationships.
Careers.
What is important and what is not. Everything changed, but something stayed the same.

Checking the address on the envelope she stood again on the sidewalk outside that strange place from long ago. The glass, the brass, the rays of light on marble floor; The Exchange.

"Ah, so good to see you again!" Reading glasses and pinstripe suit the same as before.

"You remember me after all this time?" She certainly remembered him.

"Of course! Have you decided to accept The Invitation? To come into The Exchange?"

"Well, things change. Perhaps. What is in there?" peering past him, toward the opening.

"All you've ever hoped for, in ways you never expected. May I escort you?" pointing to a revolving door that now stood motionless, partition open to the sidewalk.

The room was bright. Shafts of glimmering, sunlit rays bounced off the dust in the air that was streaming down from the light in the dome. Golden, rich auburn and amber hues strewn themselves across the room. An autumn palate of marble counters, mahogany wood, accents of gold fixtures. Clerks, men and women at writing tables, everywhere all the markings of wealth, stature, and purpose, grandeur even.

"I don't belong here," she mused to herself as she scanned the room.

"But you have an invitation." Pinstripe stepped aside, closer to her, as others came in through the door.

"It was a mistake. Wrong person. An error," she muttered as she turned toward him.

"I don't think so, it had your name on it, Lydia." A gentle smile crossed the corners of his mouth, then broadened to his graying temples as he looked toward her hand, "Still does."

She hadn't realized that she was still clutching the rumpled envelope; looking down as she unfolded it, her name was still there.

"What is this place?" she whispered as her pretense dropped to the floor.

Patiently, peace filling the space, Pinstripe leaning in, "This is The Exchange. You give what you have and gain all that there is."

Questions flooded her mind, swirling against her framework of understanding. "Focus, focus, focus," she told herself. What was she doing here? Why was she invited? What should she do? What was really required? It was way too good to be true.

Therefore...

it

had

to

be

False!

She stood still;—but where's the catch? Looking, processing, trying to find a place in her mind, her experience, where any of this made sense.

"Well, you don't know anything about me—what I've done, who I am, what I want . . ." her voice trailing off as she continued to look around, finally landing on the face of Pinstripe.

Putting his hand on her shoulder, "I don't need to; you have an invitation."

Recent experiences had taught her to be wary, to leave trust at the door and not let it enter her heart. And yet something was seeping in, flowing gently through the cracks of her reasoning, what was this? A long ago, familiar feeling; what was it, where had she felt this before?

"So, what do I do?" she whispered. A shift, a flow, a sense, what was this!? Reason tried to slam the door, but she still felt something else slipping in. What was this feeling? Truth? Hope? Light? Courage?

"Follow me, I'll show you." Doubt falling off in a trail behind her, she walked to the table in the center of the room and watched as a man across from her nervously filled in a slip and walked toward a clerk.

CHAPTER 4

The Introduction

John

It was getting more comfortable, more real, more tangible, this Exchange. He tapped his cap toward the pinstriped suit who then nodded back as he entered the revolving doors. Always light, always golden, always streaming, that's what John had come to expect. Each time, each exchange. Reliable, predictable.

The song in his head started coming through his vocal chords and a well-known tune hummed out. His table, his favorite writing table, was only slightly occupied by a woman and a man; as the man strode off to the clerk, John noted to himself, "First-timer." The woman was watching everything, scanning the room, "Newcomer."

He'd become adroit, accustomed, familiar with the process. Putting his keys into his pocket, as he went to a different table, he grabbed a pen and filled out the slip. Handing his slip to the clerk, he received his envelope. It was always the same, the contents, always more than enough, more than he needed, more than he dared ask. He never used all of it, wasn't quite sure how. Even now, he mused, "How can this all be?" Bit by bit, he had given himself away. Things were different now, he understood more, he knew a few of the regulars, and, touching his cap, said hello. The routine.

Looking back toward the door, he noticed something new. Really? Something new, or had he just not noticed before. Putting the pen down, he glanced past the woman standing at the table to the corner arrangement of chairs, lush rug, and fireplace.

Fireplace?

Why had he never noticed that before? The warmth stretched even to the center of the room, the popping and crackling became a rhythm in the background. Sweeping the room, he looked for others who had noticed, seen the new thing. No one stopped, no one stared, no one turned aside. "Huh," he said to himself, "Wonder what that is?" There was some distance from the table to the corner, no one headed that way, no one disturbed the couple in conversation. He felt a pull, a tug hauling the liner to the ocean, his heart wouldn't let it go. "I'm fine," he mused. "This is the routine. I have more than I know what to do with. Stay the course, John, stay the course." Yet . . . the draw to the corner compelled him to move.

One more glance around the room as he started toward the corner, watching the couple finish their conversation. He noticed the old woman's lingering touch on the arm of the distinguished gentleman as she arose walking toward the door; leaving behind someone he had never seen before. Who was *that* man? He thought he knew everyone, the regulars, the clerks, the managers, the staff. Who was this? Their touch was that of close companions, intimate even. That realization discomfited him.

Resting comfortably near the fire, the gentleman's eyes locked on John. His gentle smile and hand wave beckoned John closer.

"Have a seat. I've been waiting for you." The gentleman rose, shook John's hand and gestured to the waiting wingback.

"Really? You work here?" John asked, settling himself into the leather and putting his feet up on the footrest.

"You could say that, although my work is everywhere, I enjoy being around."

"Well, I ain't never seen you here before." Taking his cap off and rubbing his hands through his sandy hair, his mind wandered, 'Where did he leave his slip? Back at the table?'

"I'm always visible to those who notice."

The fire certainly was comforting, he didn't remember needing to be comforted, but still it felt good. Warm, bright, flickering, he stared intently into the flame, becoming curious—where were the logs? No stack of firewood stood nearby, no gas line fed the flame, no fuel that he could see;

just beautiful, undulating flame. Hmmm . . . this was new, the gentleman was new, the fire was new, The Conversation was new.

John didn't care for new.

"Well, I've been here a bit. A regular, so to speak. Always doing my part, giving what I can, well, really only what I want to give." He leaned in and gave a wink. "No demands. Nice, clean exchange."

"And have you found the return to be adequate?"

"Yes, the rate of return is really good." Returning his cap to his head, he added, "Actually, a bit too good. It's way beyond what I need—haven't found a good place or purpose for all of it yet. Not concerned, though, got what I want."

"Oh, that's interesting. What are your thoughts about that?" the gentleman leaned back crossing his legs, his arms at rest.

"Don't know what to think. Guess I'm grateful, appreciate the process. So far, doesn't ask too much, seems pretty straightforward; a rather simple exchange."

"Yes, I understand your perspective, I believe. If that's all you want, then you are pretty well satisfied. You understand the rules, and are getting along quite fine."

"Yep, that's about it. What about you? Is the return good for you?" Readjusting his cap.

"Hmmm, is the return good for me? Am I getting all that I ever hoped for, all that I ever asked?" musing to himself while peering at the man with the cap. *"Interesting question. Do you ever wonder if this is it? If this is all there is to The Exchange?"*

Leaning in just a bit closer, looking around, then adjusting himself back into the wingback, the capped man said softly, "Yeah, yeah, I do. I mean, what's the catch? I give what I want, what I have, and in return get all that I ever dreamed of. Like I said, I don't know what to do with it all." Leaning further back into the chair, he continued, a little louder, "But I come all the same. Seems the right thing to do, you know?" He looked around the room.

"Would you be interested in knowing how to invest your return? What to do with it? Are you curious about what can be done? About something more?"

"Maybe. You know I've got it pretty good right now. Good routine, good process; I know what's going on. If there's more to it, I just don't know about something new, something I haven't tried before," he rambled. "I'm pretty comfortable, just curious a bit, you see?" Glancing around The Exchange, "Just wondering, if this is it, you know. Like I just saw you sitting here in the corner and wondered, you know?" Turning back toward the man, "Just, like, so what if there is something more." Then glancing over to the door, "That's a risk, like, you know, a risk! What if it doesn't work out?"

"What if it does?" Settling himself further in his chair, hands clasped resting under his chin, the man smiled at John, *"What if it does?"*

CHAPTER 5

The Conversation

Lydia, Part 3

She came often, even felt compelled to come, to attend. The Exchange was always open, the door always revolving, the people coming and going. The sunlit rays from the dome above beamed into the marble, putting everything in an amber glow. The rich warmth of the wood and gold were expected, known, familiar now. Recently, the fire in the corner is what brought her back. She already had everything that she had ever hoped for, all that she dreamed of. She was in need of nothing. Yet she was becoming more and more aware that she needed everything.

He waited for her, at their place, their corner of The Exchange. He was always there; others didn't seem to notice, but she did. She knew he was there, waiting for her, just her. Her anticipation arose to meet him again, to The Conversation. The comfort, warmth, wisdom, gentleness—almost shy, overwhelmingly secure, and confident, the person by the fire, in the wingback chair. Beyond introduction, they now were friends, or was it mentor, or partner, or . . . how could she describe their relationship? Who was he? So different, so intelligent with no ambition, so accomplished with no arrogance; just calm, rest and peace by the fire. Although she knew so little about him, she loved their time, their conversation; nothing like it existed with anyone else.

"How are you today, my dear Lydia?" clasping her hand with his, then he gestured toward the vacant chair, her chair, her place by the fire.

"Well." She settled into her chair.

"Yes?"

How did he know, how did he always know when it wasn't quite the truth, or the whole of it?

"Well, I am concerned about something."

"Concerned?"

Again, she marveled, how did he know?

"Well, beyond concerned, I guess; worried actually. Yes, that would be it, I'm worried."

"Really! About what are you worried? You have everything."

"My investments. I'm not sure I'm doing enough. I'm not sure I'm smart enough or accomplished enough, or even know enough to manage them well. I don't, I don't,...I don't think I'm up to it. It's a lot, you know, a lot to manage well. How do I know if it will perform, if it's good enough of a strategy?" The flurry of words spilling out of her, a waterfall of anxiety.

"Ah, you are worried that you are not enough." He leaned forward, *"Who told you that you weren't enough?"* Looking at her intently, *"Where did you acquire that information? What is the evidence that your investment has returned poorly?"*

What she wanted was the comforting side of him, the consoler of her woe, she wanted a sympathetic ear, reassurance that he would make it alright. She was anxious, worked up even, fear had made itself a home. What if she hadn't done things right?

What was this about information, evidence? Yet she saw no condemnation, no chastisement, no ridicule for her feelings, nor did he assuage them. What was this response? How should she answer without appearing foolish for her worry, her concern? How could she respond without losing his high regard? Her position in his eyes?

Patiently, he waited. His demeanor of respect, trust, calmness, and gentleness settled into the space. As the silence lingered, she formulated her response. Would she lose his respect if she answered foolishly? If he saw her as she saw herself?

"I'm just anxious, that's all. I'm sorry."

"What are you sorry for?"

"Oh, for bringing it up, just for being foolish, I guess. I still have everything, even if I invest it poorly, I still have more than I ever dreamed."

Settling back into his chair, crossing his legs, his arms at rest, *"Is it that you have everything, or is it what you believe about having everything?"*

Initially stunned by this question, she realized that this is what she valued and loved most about their time together. He knew. He really knew what the core was, what the heart of the matter was. His wisdom cut through her emotions, rending yet healing, the truth exposed.

*"Do you truly **believe** that you will always have more than you can dream already?"*

In the silence, the fire popped, flaming high, warmth flowing freely. Light streamed through the dome above, it was always high noon in The Exchange. Time slowed around her as she considered: What did she believe about having everything she ever dreamed of. She had done nothing to obtain it. All she did was respond to the Invitation. Could she lose it when it had been given to her freely? If she would always have everything, was it even possible to lose anything?

Her early trips to The Exchange told her that, no matter what she gave, she would always receive everything. Would she lose his affection, his high regard if she invested poorly? Was this the true cause of her anxiety? Was her concern for the investment, or for his approval, his regard, even love toward her? Would their time together cease because she performed poorly, or didn't live up to all that he invested in her?

Was she enough?

She pondered, unsure of the answer, unwilling to risk a response that wasn't correct. Glancing across the room, past the elevator, she noticed for the first time a children's area with puzzles, toys, books, and stuffed animals popping out of gaily colored boxes. So different from everything around her. Sitting in a small rocking chair, a little girl held a doll while turning the pages of a book. "Oh, to be like *that* again! No worries, no concerns about the right answer, no responsibilities, no dilemmas," she thought. "Oh, to be as a child," she whispered.

Watching her gaze across the room, he broke the silence, *"Perhaps your answer lies there."*

CHAPTER 6

The Garden

Andras, Part 2

Pushing out the revolving door he burst onto the sidewalk, envelope in hand. "What just happened?" He looked back through the glass, the brass, past the man with the pinstripe suit and saw the amber glow of the lobby of the Exchange streaming back. People came and went, in and out, in and out . . . the door rotating rhythmically with all the action. He stared at the envelope, beautifully calligraphed, his name was in a bold hand.

"Freaky, huh?" from the teenager kicking back his skateboard.

"What?"

"Legit, though, real legit. I come here all the time", as the teen stopped outside the door.

"YOU come here?"

"Yeah, just said that didn't I? Couldn't do without it now. Addicted, like, only good."

"You come here *all* the time?" Andras' mouth dropping, eyebrows raised.

"Slow, you are real slow, man." Speaking slower, "Yes, daily; sometimes more, sometimes less; pretty much daily. I bet this is your first time, huh?"

"Well . . ., I . . ., I mean, uh. Yes, first time." Andras wondered who was this boy?

"You'll get used to it, you'll figure it out." Turning away, Elias leaned his skateboard against the glass wall, fist bumped the pinstripe suit and walked inside.

"What is going on?!" Andras realized that he hadn't talked to a teenager in years. He had been one once, he remembered, but that was a long time ago. Cares and responsibilities ago.

Across from the Exchange was a park, he'd noticed it before but never bothered to go in and explore. A beautiful flower garden of roses, lilies, and dahlias exploded in color as he found a bench and sat down. Fountains of flowing water, trees in full array, the bench sat under a canopy of shade and bloom. He'd picked up a coffee to steady his nerves from the outdoor kiosk, now he sat with his envelope beside him, deep in ponder, thought . . . wonder.

"Can I help you?" said the voice. He looked so amiable, so open, so different, as he stood next to the bench.

"Oh, do you work here?" putting his cup down he tried to stuff the envelope into his coat pocket as he started to get up.

"Oh, it's okay, you can sit here, that's what it's for." The Gardener's eyes gave a wink.

"Well, let's say I'm always around, doing what needs to be done."

Unaccustomed to talking with strangers, which was anyone that he didn't know, which he now realized was most everyone, he couldn't resist The Invitation of the voice. "Yes, okay." Andras stammered, " I never walked in this park before; it's beautiful, I mean, like, really beautiful; everything is in bloom, there's so much color, the leaves . . ." realizing that he was rambling, he stopped.

"May I join you on the bench," the Gardener cocking his head slightly.

"Sure, yes, help yourself." Scooting as far over as he could, he made ample room for the other to sit down.

"Just come from The Exchange?"

"Yes. Yes, I did."

Putting his tools down beside him, he kept on, *"And I am guessing it was your first time? First-timers often end up here, in The Garden."*

Looking the Gardener over, trying not to stare, "**You** seem to know about it." How could this guy know anything about it? Did he go there? He seemed so, so . . . normal. The jeans, the boots, and garden gloves. Turning so that he could see him straight on, he realized that The Gardener's hands were dirty with soil; his sleeves, rolled up, exposing long, tanned arm muscles; and the face, while only middle aged, was full of expressive lines from years in the sun.

Leaning back, crossing his feet as he stretched his long legs in front of him, *"Well yes, I have been with many people from The Exchange. I myself went there once. Would you mind if I looked at your invitation, Andras?"*

"How did you know my name!"

"Well, I saw it on your envelope when you put it in your pocket, so I know it's on your invitation," he said with a large grin. *"It's okay, if you don't want to show me."* The Gardener shifted position and turned toward the man with his right arm on the back of the bench.

"I know that this has all been a bit strange and you are a very ordered person, so doing something unusual is uncomfortable." He paused, a slight breath exhaled. *"Risk-taking is something you don't do lightly; you are careful with your investments. That caution has accomplished great wealth. What brought you to The Exchange wasn't curiosity, you were looking for an answer to a problem. A problem so complex and personal that you couldn't solve it on your own, although you certainly tried. You needed help. The Invitation came and you felt you were at a point you would try almost anything."*

Andras stood so quickly he appeared to jump. In his eyes, a mix of surprise and alarm darted around the now empty park, finally landing on The Gardener. He could not understand what was happening. "Who are you?" flew from his lips as he threw the envelope on the ground and quickly walked away.

CHAPTER 7

The Last Visit

Gray Hair

She knew it was her last visit.

There was nothing left to exchange; her final deposit made.

They lingered by the fire, her last conversation in The Exchange. Arising, she touched his arm, with great appreciation and love; she knew that her time was full.

She wrapped her hair in her favorite scarf, pulled her coat around her and headed past the elevator, toward the door. Glancing behind her, a man ambled toward the chairs by the fire,... her chair, ...her place that she had occupied so many years. Walking by the children, her heart reached out, remembering all she had experienced in her time with them.

Yes, she was satisfied, fully satisfied.

Peace filled her and flowed out, filling the air around her with perfume.

Now all that was left was her last stroll through the park.

Everything exchanged, everything received.

Her last visit to The Exchange.

CHAPTER 8

Golden Exchange

E velyn, Part 1

"Hello. Hello. Hello!" her sing-song greeting increased in laughter and intensity with each step as she walked toward the revolving door.

A large smile creating creases around his eyes, the pin-striped man grinned at the woman. She was positively gold-en! From her blonde hair, flowing graciously around her face, to her bracelets, rings, dress and shoes. Golden. Even the ivory sweater she pulled off, stuffing it into her bag, echoed the gilded exuberance.

"Hello to you, ma'am!"

"Well, I have it here somewhere," rummaging through her blue satchel. Looking up, "Oh, I'm sorry, I'm assuming that I'm in the right place, I've seen it here and always wondered. Then, the other day, this came," still working her way through the crowded bag: the keys, her purse, the samples, the mail, contracts, fabrics. "Oh, It's here someplace. I'm sorry, I should have had it out. Oh!" as she pulled out the calligraphed envelope, untangling papers, folders, and clips.

"Yes, ma'am. Found what you were looking for I assume?" Pinstripe grinning as far as his lips would spread.

Closing her leather bag and stepping back, she laughed. "Oh, I was in such a hurry that I didn't even greet you! How are you today? I'm so glad to meet you!"

And he believed that to be true.

Picking up her pace, Pinstripe exclaimed, "Well. I'm well. Especially today; always a great day to meet someone new."

"Ha! New? Well, that's terrific, I love being new! All things new I say! So much going on!" Her song continued.

"Welcome to The Exchange," he said, eyeing the envelope. "Something new today for you, I believe."

"Yes! I've got so many things going on, but this came, and I wondered what it was all about. It seemed important, so I squeezed it in between appointments."

The revolving door opened behind him, "Excuse me, please," to the golden woman, "for just a moment." Pinstripe stepped aside to assist the graying woman emerging from

The Exchange. "Goodbye," he said, grasping her small veined hand in his and looking into her beaming face.

"Yes, it is. Thank you." The old woman lingered a moment, "Thank you for everything. Fare well." smiling up at him, she made her way across the street to the park.

Seeing his conversation was over with the older woman, Evelyn asked the doorman, "So! What is this place? Should I just go in? Only I've got so many people lined up today. I help people, here's my card, in case you know anyone who needs help. Help with design, I mean, that's what gives me joy!" Once again, she delved into the beautiful blue bag, producing a fashionable card with raised gold lettering, "Evelyn's Designs."

CHAPTER 9

Deserted Exchange

Evelyn, Part 2

Emerging from The Exchange, she stopped on the sidewalk and tore into the golden envelope.

"AH!" she cried.

"OH!" joy celebrating around her.

"Oh, wow, oh *wow* . . . This is marvelous! I could never have imagined this!" She walked toward the park with the envelope in her hand. The greenery, trees, and blossoms spread out before her, she felt like she was in the beginning of all there ever was. Joy, bliss, wonder flowed through her as she examined the contents of her exchange. "Wow . . ." she whispered to herself.

She walked past the group of teens and a man talking excitedly, exclamations shooting out from their conversation. Reading and rereading the contents of her envelope, "What luck!" she thought. Looking up she recognized where she was and headed toward the park bench, the one under the shade of the large birch tree. Near it, The Gardener was raking leaves from the surrounding beds. She'd seen him before, but it wasn't like she stopped to talk to the workers, unless of course it was **her** workers. On the path she saw an influential client making his way toward her. He was one of her favorites. Always at the front end of design, he had referred many her way, and she had benefited greatly from their relationship.

"Evelyn, Evelyn! So good to see you!" Although it was late summer, his scarf, hat, and coat pointed to the cold winter ahead.

"Oh! Always a delight! You'll never guess where I've been!" She shifted her leather bag to her shoulder, freeing both hands to show him the envelope.

The client took the envelope and, without looking it over, "I've seen these before."

"Oh really!? Have you gone inside The Exchange?"

"No! Of course not! What nonsense, what foolishness is this? Are you participating in this, this, this Exchange?" he said, looking at the envelope in disbelief. She was always so cutting edge, how could she be interested in something so passe, so simplistic, so discounted in today's social circles?

"Well, I . . . I got The Invitation, and I thought I'd try it. Is there something wrong, it looks so amazing!" Her joy disappeared with each word.

"I can tell you that anyone who associates with The Exchange is no acquaintance of mine. I will not patronize any group, any person, any business who associates with such foolishness," handing back the envelope with a thrust of his hand.

"Oh, well, of course not. I just wanted to see what it's all about; just curious, I guess," as she dropped the envelope and its contents in the nearby garbage bin.

"Well, see that your curiosity doesn't get the cat. You know what I mean?"

"Yes, I do." As they walked away, she turned back and saw The Gardener leaning on his rake, watching her, compassion in his eyes.

CHAPTER 10

The Report

Pinstripe's Day

"Yes, sir. She did, sir." Pinstripe had stepped through the revolving doors and inside The Exchange, his daily task before him.

The Report.

"She did stop today, though; she looked, that's something. It means that she still knows she's invited, and every day she does come by." The smile of his eyebrows arching over the reading glasses.

"Yes, I smile, she smiles, and then she goes on." Then a sigh, a moment shared between them.

"Oh, yes, the boy, Elias. What a delight! He's learning to leave the skateboard outside, such a bright one. Comes in daily now. Today he came twice!" Nodding his head, in agreement, "Ah, visiting the fireplace now is he? And he did connect with Andras. Yes, I thought that was a benefit as well. Andras does need that and I will mention it the next time he visits. So glad he stopped by today! He only recently received his invitation. A quick response is always promising." The effusive words tumbling out. A pause. Turning his head, rubbing his eyes with one hand, his glasses in the other, slower, "Oh, I see. Hmm . . . well, perhaps another invitation can be extended?"

As The Report went on, the pinstriped man relaxed and settled deeply into the cushioned chair. His glasses came off and on, alternating with the punctuation of each person involved. The crackle of the fireplace in the background, the daily routine, the comfort of knowing and being known. How he loved this time of the day. Handing the door off to his evening counterpart, coming into the quiet order of The Exchange, always a little slower this time of day. Fascinated with the glow of the light inside and the shuttering of the day outside; his daily report, sharing the joy of those who visited and the hope for those who didn't.

CHAPTER 11

The Diversion

D_{allin}

His backpack hung over a shoulder; keys, dangling from the blue carabiner, hitting the water bottle rhythmically as he approached the building. Curiosity and challenge. He would figure out what this Invitation was all about, and he'd do it right now. His next class was in an hour, and this shouldn't take that long.

Flashing his Invitation to the pinstriped man outside, he pushed through the revolving door and into the atrium of The Exchange. Light falling through shafts of the dome catching the air, he took a quick look around. "Hmpph, looks like a bank," he thought. He walked up to what looked like a clerk behind a window.

"Hi. New here; got this invitation, wondering what this is all about." His clipped speech revealing the hurry.

The balding man behind the counter cocked his head, squinted his eyes, and said, "Yes, this is The Exchange. You exchange all that you have and receive more than you ever dreamed of."

"Yah, well, how does that work?" His thought bubble: this is SO bogus! His foot involuntarily started tapping the marble floor.

"Well, what do you have?" the clerk, now curious himself.

"I'm a student; what do you think I have? A few student loans, some books, a laptop, hiking boots, that's about it."

"Yes, those are what you possess, but what do you have? You, yourself, who you are?"

"I don't get it." Looking at his phone for the time, he glanced around and thought, "What a *waste* of time . . ."

In spite of the obvious brush, the clerk continued, "Each of us has something of our own, something given to us specifically. Our will, our hopes, our experiences, our emotions, those things that make you, uniquely you. This is what you exchange."

"Oh wow," clarity crossing his face. "I'm a chemical engineering major, I don't do this stuff," he announced walking toward the door.

"The Exchange is always open . . ." the clerk's words falling behind him as Dallin pushed the revolving door.

Heading toward the park across from The Exchange, he knew that he could clear his mind a bit as he walked through. As Dallin passed The Gardener he slipped his arm through the rest of the backpack and breathed deeply the freshness of the park in the midst of the city. On the park road, he noticed the city garbage truck was emptying bins. As he walked by the truck, the garbage hauler said, "Got some trash? I'm picking up now."

"Yep," replied the engineering major, dropping The Invitation into the bin on the truck's mechanical arm.

CHAPTER 12

Busy Day

P_{hilip}

"Ah, there he is!" The man in the pinstripe suit looked toward the park, recognizing a familiar figure.

Philip.

"Yes, it's going to be a busy day," Pinstripe mused.

Philip crossed the road to the park as the noise of the weekly garbage pick-up diminished in the distance. His eyes glancing around, he noticed The Gardener adjusting the water lines near the bench. Philip patted his back and The Gardener stood up for a quick hug, "It's a good day. A busy day." Philip winked in response.

"Hey, did you get an invitation?" Philip called out. "Did you lose yours? I have more!" The teens were gathered around the park gazebo, one of them looked up at the man coming toward them.

"Invitation to what?" the redhead responded.

"Oh, so good! So much more than you expect! Better than you can imagine!"

"I don't know; I can imagine quite a bit," a smirk crossing the redhead's face, laughter erupting from the group.

Clearly the leader, Philip noted the teens all looked toward the redhead as he talked.

"Did you get one of these?" Philip took an ivory envelope with golden writing embossed on the front out of his coat pocket and showed it to the group.

A series of *yeah*s, *yes*es, and *yep*s could be heard, complete with heads nodding all around.

"Well, let me tell you more about it . . ." Philip stepped closer as the group parted to give him room.

The Exchange door revolving beside him, "Well, well, here they come." Pinstripe looked across the road at a group of teens excitedly talking amongst themselves, making their way to The Exchange, Philip and a redheaded boy leading the way.

CHAPTER 13

Cultivating

The Gardener

The Gardener loved soil. He loved to scoop a pile of fresh mulch and run it through his fingers. He loved digging in the hard earth until it crumbled in his palm. He loved soil. He loved what it did; how, with just a little bit of water and a little bit of care, out of it came all types of growing things.

He noticed that was true of the people who came through the park. A little bit of water, a little bit of care, and all kinds of goodness would grow. Nothing escaped his eye; his gaze on everything and everyone. He loved it when people visited; he could see tension, fear, shame drain away under the freedom of the trees in the wind, the flowers array of color and the glistening of the water. No greater joy did The Gardener have than the enjoyment of those in his park.

He knew every inch of the park. He, himself, had built the benches, the fountains, the gazebo, the paths. He, himself, had carefully plotted out the many gardens, arbors, and groves, thoughtfully combining color, size, and texture for constant display. He'd worked there forever, and he wanted to spend all eternity there. In The Garden, where everything and everyone grew.

Today there was much activity. The full spectrum of joy, discovery, rejection, pain, belonging; being human in his garden. He'd made sure that he was near when those at the bench needed a word. He'd made sure to step aside when Philip was in full bloom, knowing the enjoyment he had talking to others about their Invitation. He'd made sure to be nearby, even when decisions made by others caused sorrow. He was everywhere that he needed to be and did everything that was needed by others. He had devoted his life to it, to making a beautiful, flourishing, garden, creating a way to The Exchange.

CHAPTER 14

The Conversation of More

Elias, Part 1

Elias loved, loved, *loved* coming to The Exchange. He noticed that more kids his age, and younger, too, were starting to show up. He knew there were older ones, but he didn't tend to pay a lot of attention; he'd grow old, too, some day, and then he'd notice.

Guiding his skateboard through the park, he waved exuberantly at The Gardener, loving the feeling of being known, of belonging. He knew, deeply knew, that he, Elias, belonged wherever he was! As he crossed the street, he waved at the man in the pinstripe suit standing aside from the revolving door. "Love that guy!" he muttered to himself. The door-man didn't notice the wave; he was engaged with a beautiful woman in a golden glow.

"Ha! First timer! Good for her!" Elias thought.

"Afternoon!" Elias yelled as he kicked the skateboard up into his waiting hand.

"Yes, it is!" greeted the doorman, the golden woman now inside, "Yes, it is."

After putting his skateboard outside on the wall, left of the door, he went over for his daily chat with the doorman. "This guy knows SO much," he thought.

After a few customary comments about who was coming in and who was looking, "Hey, here comes Philip!"

"Well, well, here they come." A broad smile, eyes lighting up his face, the doorman bent at the waist and ushered the group in with a bow.

Philip waving as he passed, Elias turned back to the man in the pinstripe suit, "You see everything, man, everything!"

"Well, everything here. Everything important here."

Elias walked through the revolving door into The Exchange. He loved that door! So cool, to walk in step, auto-matically entered, welcomed in. Glancing across the room, he saw everything familiar in one glance: The streaming rays of sunlight, even though it was late afternoon. The clerks in their stations, efficient, knowing, taking the exchange of everyone there. Confidentially discreet. Full of people, yet no lines. Those at the tables deciding their exchanges, new and old, one by one, engaged in the process of life. Over at the fireplace, he saw a man with a cap in deep conversation. "Ah, he thought, that's his first time there. I wonder what he's thinking?" Sweeping to the right, he saw the children's area. He'd seen it before but had never gone over there. That was below him; he didn't need to play with the kids.

Waving to the clerks, who all glanced up in sync and nodded, he looked over to the fireplace. The man in the cap was rising, adjusting his suspenders, and walking toward the door. Glancing around, he noticed that no one was waiting, and he headed over to the favorite part of his day, to The Conversation.

Although he wasn't cold, the crackling and warmth of the fire always comforted him. He walked up to the fire and grinned at the man across from him.

"Hey!"

"Hey," he smiled. *"So good to see you, so very good. I was expecting you."*

How did he always know? No matter when Elias showed up, he always knew, always expecting.

"I have an invitation for you today." Settling back into his chair, his eyes smiled playfully, yet his face set in the seriousness of the offer, his hand gesturing to the opposite chair. Elias's chair. "Really? An invitation? To what? I mean, I've exchanged lots of times. You know, I'm here all the time. I know how this works," chattering away as he sat down, settling himself deep in the cushion for The Conversation.

"You know how some of it works. But the deeper ways are yet unknown to you." There was a pause, and he continued, *"This is an invitation to enter into becoming The Beloved."* At this comment, the fire flared up and popped loudly, the clerks all glancing in sync to the fireplace and The Conversation there.

"*This is an exchange like no other. It's an exchange from which there is no return. An exchange offered only to those at the point of This Conversation are ready.* He paused. *You are at that point.*"

A dense layer of gravity descended on Elias. He understood the seriousness of the offer. They had never talked this way before. But now, in this moment, he knew there was **more**. What he had never seen before, he now connected back. The clues at the fireplace leading to this one place, this exact point in time. The ultimate exchange. The *more* that he had never considered before came to him as a possibility. But what was the cost? He thought back to his many exchanges. In recent days, he had given all he had, but now wondering, had he really? What had he held back? What remained?

CHAPTER 15

The Exchange for More

Elias, Part 2

Silence settled in as Elias pondered. He knew the man did not enter The Conversation lightly, nor did he engage in diversion tactics. Elias's next response would go somewhere, was he ready for where it went? The man waited patiently, as he studied Elias's face. Elias nervously twisted the key hanging around his neck as his mind raced in thought, 'What was this about? What does it mean to 'become the Beloved?' The truth dawned on him! He knew. He *knew* the choice. He **knew** the exchange. A deep sigh escaped as he pondered this revelation. This invitation to *more*, to becoming *The Beloved*.

Patiently, the man waited. Closely watching Elias as the light of understanding came on him. As he weighed the options in his mind.

Finally, "Is this a one-time offer? Can I think about it some more? Consider the consequences, you know?" matching the intensity of the moment, feeling a little desperate for more time, some delay in accepting The Invitation. Today was not convenient.

Carefully, the man responded, *"This offer is for now, for today, as long as it is today."* Elias wondered; how did he always know what he was thinking?

"It is possible this offer may come around in the future, but the future isn't for you to know. The cost would be different then, as you would be different then."

Now, now was the time. Accept The Invitation **and** the consequences. Take the leap, there was no going back. Stand in place, and who knew if this opportunity would come again. Looking toward the revolving door, weighing his options, he saw the darkness of the evening pass through the glass. Inside, always sunny, always, brilliantly, high noon.

"Can I come back to this place, even if I don't accept The Invitation?"

"Yes, yes you can. It will be different, however. The Invitation, once offered, changes you, changes your exchange. Once offered, there is no return to time and experience as once understood. From this point, you are changed, whether you move forward or maintain your place.

Why was this so hard!? He'd never been cheated here. He'd never experienced anything other than all that he'd ever dreamed of. To find out there was *more*, more to dream, more to all of this was exciting. Enticing even. An adventure!

But . . . it required everything.

All of him.

He understood now that he'd never actually given all he had. What would happen if he gave *all*? Nothing in reserve, nothing for himself. All. It was like dying to everything he was and knew without knowing what would become of him. He knew what was, but he didn't know what could be. Remembering the day when he made his first exchange, the same trust, the same faith arose within him. The memory of walking through that door the first time, the wonder of receiving the envelope from the clerk. The reliability of the process, the dependability, the return. What once was the ultimate leap of faith, had now become a ritual, a daily routine. Exchanges had become so easy he stopped thinking about them.

And now, he knew. Everything had changed.

Rising from his chair, he slowly took the key chain from his neck. With one last look, he folded the key in his hands and, walking over to the man with the outstretched hand, he said, "Here, this is yours."

With every step toward the children, Elias felt the weight of the decision fall behind. Each step bringing him closer to their laughter; waves of peace, joy, and love flowing into him. His first steps of becoming The Beloved.

PART 2

The Parable of the Seed

The Allegory Explained

CHAPTER 1

The Parable of the Seed

The Exchange is an allegory based on Jesus's parable of the seed. In His life, Jesus taught them many things by using stories, parables, to illustrate spiritual truths:

> *"Consider this: There was a farmer who went out to sow seeds. As he cast his seeds, some fell along the beaten path and the birds came and ate them. Others fell onto gravel that had no topsoil. They quickly shot up, but when the days grew hot, they were scorched and withered because they had insufficient roots. Others fell among the thorns, so when they sprouted, the thorns choked them. But other seeds fell on good, rich soil that kept producing a*

good harvest. Some yielded thirty, some sixty, and some even one hundred times as much as he planted! If you're able to understand this, then you need to respond."

Then his disciples approached Jesus and asked, "Why do you always speak to people in these hard-to-understand parables?"

He explained, "You've been given the intimate experience of insight into the hidden mysteries of the realm of heaven's kingdom, but they have not. For everyone who listens with an open heart will receive progressively more revelation until he has more than enough. But those who don't listen with an open, teachable heart, even the understanding that they think they have will be taken from them.

Now you are ready to hear the explanation of the parable of the sower:

What was sown along the path represents the one who listens to the message of the kingdom but doesn't understand it. The Adversary then comes and snatches away what was sown into his heart.

The one sown on gravel represents the person who gladly hears the kingdom message, but his experience remains shallow. Shortly after he hears it, troubles and persecutions come because of the kingdom message he received. Then he quickly falls away for the truth didn't sink deeply into his heart.

The one sown among thorns represents one who receives the message, but all of life's busy distractions, his divided heart, and his ambition for wealth result in suffocating the kingdom message, and it becomes fruitless.

But what was sown on good, rich soil represents the one who hears and fully embraces the message of the kingdom. Their lives bear good fruit—some yield a harvest of thirty, sixty, even one hundred times as much as was sown." Matthew 13:3–12 and 18–23 TPT

CHAPTER 2

Seed by the Road

Andras

Andras had worked hard for everything he had. He was focused, intense, and deeply walled into himself. Interactions were meant to produce something or solve a problem. Rarely did he converse with anyone outside his work or his small, immediate group. He realized that, even within that group, his interaction was only with those he considered "productive." What did anyone really know about him?

Recent hardships had come into his life . . . pain and trouble. The pain he could contain and put in its box as he always had done, his heart a fortress against the sea. But trouble? That was another story: how to solve the situation outside of himself. Stagnant with desperation, one day The Invitation came to his desk. For the first time, he considered: Does help lay elsewhere?

No one gave him anything, especially for so little invested. Because that's what it was, an investment. He invested what he considered slight, of limited use, so that he could get more, of huge use. This exchange, this trade that he had just made gave him everything. Everything!

'This can't be,' he mused. 'When it's too good to be true, it most certainly isn't.' Yet, in his hands, was everything to solve that situation, his problem, his crisis and more. What were the strings, what did he now owe?

What had he done!

Deep within, in smallness and gray, he felt something. A spark, a word, rising up: *hope*. That was a dangerous word; he pushed it down, back where it belonged into the dungeon of the fortress of his heart. Hope only ended in pain, and he had that under control. He didn't know what The Gardener was up to, or how he had gotten so close to the truth; but it didn't matter, the walls of reason and self would protect him.

The door to his heart slammed shut.

Abruptly rising from the bench, Andras practically sprinted away from The Gardener, his brain on fire. "I do not understand, who is this guy? What gives him the right to talk to me like that!? None of this makes sense!" words of flame smoldering as he walked away.

His emotions reeling as he passed the fountain, "I did nothing. I got everything. This is too good to be true, so it isn't. There's a catch somewhere that I don't understand. Yet..." to no one but himself.

Andras's mental and emotional energies spent, he left The Garden, matching the pace of the crowd heading down the sidewalk to his office. Breathing in, "It's okay, though. I really traded next to nothing, so no loss there. I'm safe," he muttered, fingering the key safely tucked in his pocket.

"Here, then, is the deeper meaning to my parable:
The word of God is the seed that is sown into hearts.
The hard pathway represents the hard hearts of those who
hear the word of God but the slanderer quickly snatches away
what was sown in their hearts to keep them from believing
and experiencing salvation."
— Luke 8:11–12 TPT

I am a smart guy, I will figure it out on my own.
I don't need someone else to do that for me.

CHAPTER 3

Seed on Rocky Places

Evelyn

'You have to be practical about these things,' she thought. 'If it sounds too good to be true, it probably is.' Hooking her elbow into his, she walked through the park, glad to have escaped social disaster. This client was important, and she liked him, when she wasn't being intimidated by him. He did have that certain something that kept her in line. He was good for her, she reflected, good for her business, good to keep her focused, good to keep her out of trouble.

But.

But... what was in that envelope looked really good. She had felt so much joy when she opened it.

So amazing.

So, what was the word she sought? *Powerful*. She felt powerful. She felt that she could do anything, be anything. In those brief moments of belief in what the envelope contained, she had felt true, genuine joy—real joy. Not the put-on exterior that made her so winsome to clients, but deep within her; she now understood what real joy felt like. And power. Power! Always bending to the needs of her needy clients, she felt power surge through her. Power to choose, power to refuse, power to stand. Power . . . to believe. To believe that she was valued, just for herself.

Now out of the park, they walked past the revolving doors of The Exchange, across the busy street. The pinstriped man glanced at her and waved. Turning slightly toward him, her eyes met his. He knew instantly, she felt it, her choice, as his hand slowly lowered. She just met him, and yet knew his disappointment. She felt it—disappointment, hope dissolved—as she turned back to her client. Maybe there was something, but now there wasn't. Her client chattering away about his newest ideas, she turned her attention back to him, thinking, "This is where I belong, this is the one who can help me, this is who I am."

> *"The Holy Spirit is the one who gives life, that which is*
> *of the natural realm is of no help. The words I speak to you*
> *are Spirit and life. But there are still some of you who won't believe.*
> *And so, from that time on many of the disciples turned their*
> *backs on Jesus and refused to be associated with him."*
> — John 6:63, 66 TPT

I am fitted to my community, I am them.

CHAPTER 4

Seed with Thorns

Dallin

"I'm going places, but I'm not going there!" he muttered as a kid on a skateboard whizzed past him, headed straight toward The Exchange. His choice of chemical engineering, his future MBA, his curated network list; all positioned him for the rich rewards that he expected in the future. He was savvy, he was focused, he knew what he wanted: Money. Well, power was good too; but with money came power, all wrapped up in his future bow.

Glancing at his phone, he figured there was just enough time to stop by the florists and get some fresh stems for his girlfriend. He hadn't spent much time with her lately; too many classes, connections with possible investors, had made time slim. "Well, the fatness is coming," he thought, "And some flowers will show her my intent." She was a good choice for him. Her family owned a couple oil fields, they approved of his ambitions, so everything was coming together. Keeping her happy was part of the job. He was a long-term planner, and all these investments would pay off.

What was all this stuff about who you are? Bunch of psychobabble; he was ambitious, he was smart, he had a future that he could accomplish on his own. That's who he was! What is this talk about trading in who he is? Who would trade their ambition, their brains, their initiative? For what? All that I ever dreamed of? What foolishness, I am already accomplishing all that I've dreamed of, I'm making it happen. I don't need some bald guy telling me to trade in my ambition, I'm already doing that. Turning my ambition, my brain, my guts into my future. I've got it ALL handled.

> *"Listen, those of you who are boasting, 'Today or tomorrow we'll go to another city and spend some time and go into business and make heaps of profit!' But you don't have a clue what tomorrow may bring. For your fleeting life is but a warm breath of air that is visible in the cold only for a moment and then vanishes!"*
> — James 4:13–14 TPT

I am my own god, I determine my own fate.
There is nothing else, there is no need for an exchange.

CHAPTER 5

Good Soil

The Yield

> *"But what was sown on good, rich soil represents*
> *the one who hears and fully embraces the message*
> *of the kingdom. Their lives bear good fruit—some*
> *yield a harvest of thirty, sixty, even one hundred*
> *times as much as was sown."* — Matt. 18:23

In the parable of the seed, the last trio of seeds all landed on
"good" soil.

All heard...

all embraced...

all bore good fruit of the message of the Kingdom.

Yet . . .
Their yields were different.
Why?

CHAPTER 6

Thirty Yield

30

John

He knew what things were. He knew what he was about. He'd figured all this out and was good to go! Surprises? Not good. If it ain't broke, don't fix it. "Be content with what you have," that's what he always said. This was strange, though; he hadn't ever seen the fireplace, the chairs, the man; strange, maybe even weird. He didn't like weird . . . or strange. He was a straight-up man: uncomplicated, did what he was told, what was required, and that was all there was to it.

Who was this guy just sitting by a fire? He felt strange talking to this man; moving to the edge of the wingback, he was ready to leave. Warm, comforting, accepting, yes; but the world doesn't work by feeling. Glancing around, he didn't see anyone else doing it. No one standing in line, no one trying to get their place by the fire. How'd that fire work? What kept it going? And who was this man anyway? What were his credentials? Did they let just anyone come in here and act like they belonged? What were the rules about this?

The discomfort and fear of new—of change—weighed heavily on the balance of belonging, and curiosity in his mind. First one side, then the other, changing position constantly. He didn't like this, he didn't like having to think about something new, what if it was all a sham. A con job. Where was it in the rules about sitting by a fire, talking to a man—where did this fit in the policy of The Exchange? If it was allowed, then why weren't more people doing it? Don't you just show up, do your exchange, and leave? Why hang around conversing? Winning the weight of balance, the risk of change, was too great. Fearing being wrong, of the possibility of ruining the good deal he had, the decision was made. Shaking the hand of the man by the fire and walking toward the door, he knew the fire wasn't the place for him.

"The servant who received the five bags of silver began to invest the money and earned five more. The servant with two bags of silver also went to work and earned two more. But the servant who received the one bag of silver dug a hole in the ground and hid the master's money."
— Matthew 25:16–18 TPT

I'm satisfied. Whatever else there may be, it's not for me.

CHAPTER 7

Sixty Yield

60

Lydia

Was she enough? Was she doing enough?

She came often, longing to be by the fire. The actual exchange had happened, nothing new there, although she gladly followed the process. All of it, for her now, was the excuse to be by the fire, to feel the warmth, to engage her heart in The Conversation.

She did everything as correctly as she knew how. How different she was now from her first encounter. It had taken a long time to follow up on that Invitation: so much water under the bridge; her life and its issues coursing away from her. She understood much more now after the Introduction. The issues of the past were seldom a concern. Now it was all about the investment, making sure she took advantage of all that she knew and applied it well.

And yet, was she doing enough? The question haunted her, had she done everything, truly everything? Was her exchange complete, or was there something that she didn't know about—or had missed, or hadn't done correctly? Sometimes these questions haunted her, plagued her in the night.

Enough?

What more was to be done? She knew more than others, that was obvious by the nervousness of the man at the table who must have been a first timer. Lydia mused on those days, now long past. Yes, she knew things; she was good. She even brought others to The Exchange, helping them with their Invitations. She knew the staff, the process, the generosity. Yes, she was good. Yet . . .

Life was complex, she knew, managing all that was given. A lot of responsibility, her portion of work and study and keeping up with trends. She had come to a certain level of proficiency, accomplishment in her exchanges. Why then the concern of enough? He had mentioned belief, and she felt it hit her heart—a small arrow, a connection to truth. Did she really believe deep in her heart that, no matter what happened, her exchange would never be taken back? That she was now good, good enough, and even more than good? Even if she never exchanged again?

As she watched the girl with her doll and book, she wondered why she had never seen that area before. She thought she knew everything about The Exchange, yet there it now was; a children's area, a place to play, to rest. She realized that The Conversation by the fire had never led anywhere bad, was never unproductive, never without fruit or encouragement or peace. How much more might an invitation to be a child yield? Well, she must consider this later, there were other things that she must do first. Finding her keys in her purse, she leaned over to hug the man, and left as the fireplace crackled behind her.

> *"But when He, the Spirit of Truth, comes,*
> *He will guide you into all the truth; for*
> *He will not speak of His Own, but whatever he hears,*
> *He will speak . . ."*
> — John 16:13 NASB

I have so much! Is there really more?

CHAPTER 8

One-Hundred Yield

100

Elias

Each time he came, each day, Elias felt his world shift. School, job, friends—once the most important things to him gradually shifted away. Oh, he knew he still cared for those; in fact, his love of those around him had intensified. How can this be when he spent so much time in The Exchange, and so much less time in the things he once thought were most important? The weight of what comes next sat on his shoulders. College, job, Marines, trade school? But now, in this moment, he knew that none of that mattered. The light of The Exchange filled his heart, and he felt the shift of everything around him. Everything was changing, everything came into a sharp focus. A knowing. An apocalypse on his screen of life.

He'd seen the children's area before, many times; in fact, lately it had caught his attention each time he came in. But he'd really had no interest: everything was fine; in fact, better than fine just as it was. Now the lure, a fish on a hook, drew him closer and closer to that place. His mind shifted to the key that always hung around his neck, close to his heart. It guarded so much, kept him safe. It was his alone, no one had anything like it. Everyone knew him by that key, it was who he was.

Now he knew what was being asked: give his life away in the ultimate exchange. This was it—the big exchange— everything had led to this moment.

Could he give *everything*, all that he was, holding on to nothing of his own? His life, his final exchange on the line—no guarantees. He'd heard little of that new place, the place of The Beloved. Yet he had no reason to doubt. In The Exchange, everything was always way better, way more than seemed possible. 'What comes after?' he mused.

In his head, he heard the voices of others, even those in The Exchange: Reckless! A trap! False word! There is no more! Where's the proof? Too much required. Too good, it must not be true!

In his heart, Elias knew. Deep delight dawning over him, he KNEW: "I was made for this!"

> *"The person who loves his life and pampers himself will miss true life! But the one who detaches his life from this world and abandons himself to me, will find true life and enjoy it forever!"*
> — John 12:25 TPT

> *"Find your delight and true pleasure in Yahweh, and he will give you what you desire the most."*
> — Psalms 37:4 TPT

"For the Holy Spirit makes God's fatherhood real to us
as he whispers into our innermost being,
You are God's beloved child!'"
— Romans 8:16 TPT

I was made for more!

Gray Hair

Beloved.

So much time now, so much had passed, since she became The Beloved. As they sat by the fire, they reminisced on her first exchange so many years ago. Her wildness, her insecurity, her obsessions. All exchanged, all given away, and now content with everything.

At peace.

Everything she ever dreamed, hoped for, and wanted. A life lived fully as The Beloved.

Her Introduction to The Conversation came quickly once she entered The Exchange. She remembered being so eager, so full of energy, so excited to sit down to their daily time together and discover depths of wisdom she'd never dreamed of.

She was an explorer, they both knew that, and so she explored. Daily, multiple times a day even, The Conversation by the fire.

"What about . . ." "What if . . ." "Who said that . . ." "Why . . ." So many questions, so much to discover. Having found the One who could show her, teach her, and point her to the **more** with only wonderment, she entered into the children's area of The Exchange.

Now a Beloved one. Fully loved, fully known. Complete. Whole.

Filled, sated, satisfied.

Shalom.

She was The Beloved.

Her course finished, everything exchanged, everything explored. Full. Their time complete, the memories enjoyed; she rose from the chair by the fireplace for her last time in

The Exchange. She looked at the clerks, she knew all their names, they returned her smile with theirs. Walking toward the door more were coming in, 'What an adventure lay ahead,' she thought as she passed through the door one final time to the outside. Pinstripe knew; generously grasping her hand in farewell.

One last stop before she was done. The park was full of people, it was a busy, beautiful day. She knew that she'd find Him; it was never hard. He was waiting for her at the bench, their bench, under the acacia tree. Rising to greet her with a kiss on her cheek, they sat down looking at the fountain across the path. There was little to say, her heart was full. The Gardener took her veined and wrinkled hand into His, and they sat in each other's company, enjoying the Presence of stillness. Her time was complete, everything exchanged, everything learned, all fulfilled as The Beloved.

"My beloved is mine, and I am his; and his banner over me is love."
— Song of Solomon 2:4, 16 NASB

I came as a little child and became a fully mature daughter.
I have exchanged all. I am The Beloved.

CHAPTER 9

Those Who Help

Pinstripe, the Ministering Angel

How he loved his job! He was satisfied; daily satisfaction in the constant service of those coming and going to The Exchange. As long as he could remember, all the way back to creation itself, he loved his job! So many interesting people. So many lives intersecting. Such a noble and honored role to usher people into The Exchange. He was made for this, and he reveled in the fulfillment of it.

He marveled at those who came and those who didn't— those who entered and left with no exchange. He wondered how they could refuse such an offer. How could they choose another way after having seen what was available? People, humans, constantly amazed him.

And those who came and came often! What a delight to see them, to greet and welcome, to open and then close behind them. It was a privilege, he knew full well, to be part of their trades, and his joy and belonging blossomed with each one.

Mostly, prominently, pre-eminently, the time before the fire was the reward of the day. There, he was honored, respected, enveloped by the Presence of warmth and knowing. Complete and full acceptance. His thoughts and ideas heard, his heart understood, partnering with the Presence for more joy, more fulfillment in his role. He knew he brought valued information, but more than that, he deeply knew and felt it was just him, who he was, that was being honored and known. What a privilege to be here, to be part, to serve, to be full. This is what he was made for, and this was what he loved.

"What role then, do the angels have? The angels are spirit-messengers sent by God to serve those who are going to be saved."
— Hebrews 1:14 TPT

I was made for this! I was made to serve you at the door.

Philip, the Evangelist

Gathering, gathering, gathering! As he walked through the park, his eyes roamed for anyone to gather. His day started in The Conversation at the fireplace within The Exchange—the fire sending waves of warmth his way, the encouragement in the words of the seated man bringing comfort. He loved hearing about The Report from Pinstripe—who came by and who didn't. Each story brought ideas of engagement, focus, and longing. Taking notes, he formulated the plan for the day, and after an embrace, walked through the revolving doors into the sunlight. Oh! What a day!

Next stop was always to find The Gardener. He wasn't hard to find, if you knew where to look. Today his hands were in soil, deeply massaging the earth, making it ready for a new water line. The Gardener had given Philip the love of the earth, of preparation for harvest, the satisfaction of working the soil until it was ready for planting. He had learned patience in the work, all things in its time. The rhythm of sowing, watering, reaping, all part of the process he learned from The Gardener. He also learned the focus on the individual, who was ready and who wasn't. Who needed more tilling, more seeds; refreshing with water, and finally, harvest. Everything that he knew he had learned from the Master Gardener.

Phlip gave The Gardener a quick hug as He stood up from the earth, wiping His hands on dirty jeans. That was all Philip needed—a touch, a word, an acknowledgement for the day. Philip turned his gaze elsewhere. Ah! Across the park was a group of teens, gathered around the gazebo. Watching them closely for a moment, the redheaded boy drew special attention. Yes, he was the one talked about at the fire this morning, he was the leader, he was ready. Strategies to approach them flipped through the rolodex of his mind as he strode off toward the center of the park. The waterline was a sign, a good one: today would be a busy day!

> *"Philip went to look for his friend, Nathanael, and told him,*
> *'We've found him! We've found the One we've been waiting for!*
> *It's Jesus, son of Joseph from Nazareth! He's the One*
> *whom Moses and the prophets prophesied would come!'*
> *Nathanael sneered, 'Nazareth! What good thing*
> *could ever come from Nazareth?' Philip answered,*
> *'Come and let's find out!'"*
> —John 1:45–46 TPT

Do you have an invitation? Let me show you the door!

CHAPTER 10

Trinity: Son, Holy Spirit, Father

The Son, Holy Spirit, and Father all working together, all with one purpose: making man according to Their Likeness.

The Son creates the way. His life, available to all, a well-tilled garden of pleasure, delight, solace, and safety.

The Spirit draws us in. Higher, wafting through our senses. Wind-blown flame pulling to warmth, desire. A purifying fire, revealing all within.

The Father opens His Heart to all. His heart, a building so vast, a structure so sound, that all who enter are changed by its frequency.

> *"Then God said,* **'Let Us make mankind in Our image, according to Our likeness.'"**
> — Genesis 1:26 NASB

The Gardener

Jesus, the Beloved Son

I AM the True Vine. I grow in rich soil, producing a hundredfold; as I grow My many branches, they too produce—thirtyfold, sixtyfold, and even more. The ones who do not produce—with great love and care I trim them; cutting off what is unproductive, trimming back what is dead, and encouraging what will bring growth.

I AM the Way to The Exchange. I made it possible for all to enter in.

I AM the Door that opens for everyone to come to The Exchange.

I AM the Shepherd. Those that come to My field I encourage, give rest, feed, inspire, and point them all to the wealth of The Exchange.

I AM the Living Water. Fountains, rivers, and springs flow from Me to all who are thirsty.

I AM the Life. I provide life, abundant, complete, fulfilled.

I AM the Bread. I provide all that is needed to be filled and satisfied.

I AM finished with My work, and now I live to take care of all those who would come to the Exchange.

I, Myself, went to The Exchange. I traded all My inheritance, glory, and honor and accepted in exchange weakness, poverty, and frailty. I did this once. My exchange was full and complete. I gave everything that I had and received more than I ever dreamed of. My Conversation never ended as I gained wisdom and favor as The Beloved.

Now everyone can trade their weakness, poverty, and frailty for My glory, honor, and inheritance.

Now everyone can come to the comfort of the fire and learn.

Now everyone can enter in as a child and become The Beloved.

It was written of ME:

"Have this attitude in yourselves which was also in Christ Jesus,
who, as He already existed in the form of God, did not
consider equality with God something to be grasped,
instead he emptied himself of his outward glory by
reducing himself to the form of a lowly servant.
He became human! He humbled himself and became vulnerable,
choosing to be revealed as a man and was obedient"
— Phil. 2:6–8 NASB TPT

I exchanged Myself for you.
You are My exchange.

The Fire

Holy Spirit!

I AM Spirit! Those who come to Me come in spirit and gain life. I AM wholly other, not what you expect, but greater. I AM all that is good, life, joy, peace, and more. Laughter, wisdom, revelation and filling. I am unseen, until I introduce myself to those who want to join in The Conversation.

Always listening, always kind, always wise, always knowing. When I am revealed to those who come, I am their innermost connector to all they are and all We Are. Asking is all that is needed; and, in the asking, you gain—all wisdom, understanding, counsel, strength, knowledge, and awe. Endless energy, endless solace, endless belonging.

Once the exchange is made, I AM revealed to all those who want the fullness of their investment, the more, the infinite, the unseen realm. Some are content with what they do; they may come to My Warmth for the Conversation, but the spark of intimacy is a flame that they are unwilling to pursue.

Others continually come seeking the more; seeking under-standing, the comfort, the intimacy of knowing, the warmth of My Fire. Their trust is in the known, the solidness of truth, the reliability of a contained fire. And for some, this is more than enough.

But there are those . . .

Those who want a wildfire where control is no longer a friend. These hear the crackle of mystery, adventure, the beckon-ing of the unseen. The **more**. *To these an invitation is extend-ed to enter into the unpredictability of uncontained fire, to be immersed and consumed; to emerge a Phoenix of resurrection flame. To let go of everything. To turn in the key that they alone hold; to become The Beloved.*

It's been said of ME:

> *"The Spirit of Extraordinary Wisdom, the Spirit of Perfect Understanding, the Spirit of Wise Strat-egy, the Spirit of Mighty Power, the Spirit of Reve-lation, and the Spirit of the Fear of Yahweh."* — Is. 22:2 TPT

> *"He will baptize you with the Holy Spirit and fire."* — Matt. 3:11 NASB

> *"For our God is a holy, devouring fire!"* — Heb. 12:29 TPT

> *"But God now unveils these profound realities to us by the Spirit. Yes, he has revealed to us his inmost heart and deepest mysteries through the Holy Spirit, who constantly explores all things. After all, who can really see into a person's heart*

and know his hidden impulses except for that person's spirit? So it is with God. His thoughts and secrets are only fully understood by his Spirit, the Spirit of God." — 1 Cor. 2:10–11 TPT

I AM your Introduction to The Conversation to know Us More.

The Exchange

The Heart of the Father...

Daily they come to Me at My Invitation. Lovingly, I imprint their names, embossed in the gold of My Presence. All is prepared, every detail completed, at the preparation of their entrance to Me. I stand obvious, yet obscure; so prescient, yet ignored, until... they receive The Invitation for themselves.

Come, come to The Exchange, a place of receiving and responding.

Come whether you have payment or not, nothing is required, nothing is charged.

Come freely and receive all!

All you have ever wanted.

All you will ever need.

All you can dream.

Free to those who come to The Exchange!

Just one step opens the door. A first step, and a deposit for more.

I take whatever is brought, whatever is exchanged. Whatever is given, whatever is revealed. Inside, I AM always ready, always hopeful for each trade, each piece they trade and the gain of all I have ever hoped for, all I have ever dreamed.

Outside The Exchange, each one was taught there was a catch. Each one learned the knowledge of "too good to be true." Each one experienced betrayal of others and themselves. Each one knew separation, pain, and fear. Each one built their own exchange with themselves and with the world: "This is how I protect myself, and this is what I will give, and no more."

Within The Exchange we all marvel at those who come. Our delight is in each step, each written note, each word of interaction: this is what I will exchange, today. We love it when the eyes of their heart receive the exchange and the light blazes within. Our portion is the delight of their lives. My joy is their continued discovery of so good it IS true! Goodness, truth, love; a trade of little to everything, pain for joy, fear for love. Limited life to life abundant: better than they could ever hope for or dream.

I AM constant. I never change. I never give less than everything. My rate remains the same: All.

I give all, even for the smallest investment seed, I return all. All My attention. All My awareness.

All My Love.

Long ago and still now I say:

Listen! Are you thirsty for more?
Come to the refreshing waters and drink.
Even if you have no money,
come, buy, and eat.
Yes, come and buy all the wine and milk you desire—
it won't cost a thing.
Why spend your hard-earned money
on something that can't nourish you
or work so hard for something that can't satisfy?
So listen carefully to me
and you'll enjoy a sumptuous feast,
delighting in the finest of food."
— Is. 55:1–2 TPT

Come, EVERYONE who thirsts. Come to The Exchange.
Come to Me, the Great I AM!

Book 2 of
The Exchange Trilogy

I'm Ready

"I remember the first time that I pushed the button on the elevator," she said as they sat together on the bench. Taking some time to remember that moment, she tucked her gray hair further into her scarf. Looking over at Him holding her hand, she continued, "I remember it so well."

The Gardener smiled at her, opening His face wide; he squeezed her hand tighter and said, *"I do too."*

They sat there, side by side, remembering that same moment together. No need for words, their communication was perfect. The Garden's aroma in full fragrance, the splashing fountain, the serenity, entertained their senses of completion.

After a time, she whispered, "I didn't know what was coming."

"Yes."

"I didn't know how good, how much good, was ahead."

"Yes."

"Is there more, even more, now?"

"Yes. So much more. Even now."

"I'm ready. Let's go."

Helping her to her feet, The Gardener put his arm around her shoulder, pulling her close. She leaned in, as she always had.

"I am my Beloved's, and He is mine," she said as together they walked into the heart of The Garden.

"Yes, you are," The Gardener replied. *"You are My Beloved."*

> *"My lover has gone down*
> *into his garden of delight,*
> *to the flowerbeds of spices*
> *to feast with those pure in heart.*
> *I am fully devoted to my beloved,*
> *and my beloved is fully devoted to me."*
> — Song of Solomon 6:2–3 TPT

Review Inquiry

Hey, it's Alice DeWittie here.

I hope you've enjoyed the book, finding the revelation in it for you!

I have an invitation for you.

Would you consider giving The Exchange a rating and review wherever you bought the book? Let others know what *The Exchange* is about and how it impacted you.

The process is simple: go to the website of wherever you bought the book, search for my name and the book title, and leave a review.

Many thanks in advance, see you in *The Elevator!*

Alice D.

Will You Share the Revelation?

Get this book for a friend, associate, or family member!

If you have found this book valuable and know others who would be inspired, consider buying them a copy as a gift. Special bulk discounts are available if you would like your whole team or organization to benefit from reading this. Just contact info@511impact.com.

Would you like to participate in
Alice's classes and mentoring sessions
or invite her to speak to your
organization?

Contact Alice now!

Alice offers classes, mentoring, and speaking engagements.
To start a conversation, email her at: info@511impact.com.

About the Author

 Alice A. DeWittie is a passionate lover of Jesus and enjoys a life of revelation and discovery as to who He is and what He does! After serving over twenty years in leadership with public education and being involved in prayer and prophetic ministry for over thirty years, she loves to lead others into their leadership calling and prophetic destiny. Alice can be reached at: www.511impact.com.

About the Illustrator

In addition to being a full-time minister, J. Brian Craig is also a visual artist and a singer-songwriter who has released several albums of his music. He loves being able to express his faith through the arts and through curating beautiful relationships, music, design, and ideas. He resides in Torrance, California, with his wife, Dessa. They have two sons in college and a daughter just finishing up high school. Find Brian's ministry, music, and blog at: http://linktr.ee/jbriancraig.

Notes

www.ingramcontent.com/pod-product-compliance
Lightning Source LLC
Chambersburg PA
CBHW020414130626
46549CB00006B/2558